ADVISOR PREP SERIES

MULTIPLE MINI INTERVIEW FOR THE MIND

KEVYN TO, MD

Printed in the United States of America

First Edition, 2013 e.4

ISBN-10: 1-62890-863-7
ISBN-13: 9781628908633

Primedia E-launch LLC Publishing
3900 Swiss Ave
Dallas, TX 75204

Visit our websites online at:
www.mmiprepbook.com
www.advisorprepfor.me

Dedications

First and foremost,

"… to my mom and Kevin, my loving partner"

Second,

"…to my family and friends"

and last but not least,

"… to all aspiring applicants in the medical field. May God bless you in your endeavors."

Acknowledgments

"Thank you to all my students over the years for their valuable input and support"

Disclaimer

This book is presented solely for educational purposes and is not meant to be used to diagnose or treat any medical condition. For diagnosis or treatment of any medical problem, consult your own physician. The author and publisher are not offering it as legal, or other professional services advice. While best efforts have been used in preparing this book, the author and publisher make no representations or warranties of any kind and assume no liabilities of any kind with respect to the accuracy or completeness of the contents. Neither the author nor the publisher shall be held liable or responsible to any person or entity with respect to any loss or incidental or consequential damages caused, or alleged to have been caused, directly or indirectly, by the information contained herein. References are provided for informational purposes only and do not constitute endorsement of any websites or other sources. Readers should be aware that the websites listed in this book may change. This book is not intended as a substitute for live interview preparation provided for by Dr. Kevyn To.

CONTENTS

o   Dedications ... iii

o   Acknowledgements ... iv

Part 1: MMI Fundamentals

01. The Start of an Interview Revolution ... 2
02. Mmi...Mmu...Mmwhy? ... 3
03. Memoir with Dr. MMI ... 6
04. Backbone of an MMI Circuit ... 7
05. The Yes and No of MMIs ... 11
06. K.I.S.S. A.S.S. with the 5 Pockets ... 14
07. Scoring the MMIs ... 19

Part 2: Practice MMI Scenarios

08. MRI Waiting Game ... 22
09. Finding Out You have Cancer ... 27
10. Group Work Blues ... 36
11. So You Want to be a Doctor ... 43
12. Bury or Scatter? ... 48
13. A Medication Overdose ... 54
14. Same Sex Parenting ... 60
15. Opps .. I made a Mistake ... 67
16. So You Want to be a Pharmacist ... 73
17. A Not so Hot Evaluation ... 79
18. Practice Full Length MMIs ... 86

Part 3: The Extras

19. Programs that Use the MMIs ... 117
20. The Week Before: Interview Tips ... 124
21. About the Author ... 125

Part 1
MMI Fundamentals

1: The Start of an Interview Revolution

As an applicant to medical school, an envelope conveniently appeared in my mailbox from McMaster University on the same day my nephew was born. I couldn't ask for better news. I was once again an uncle and the letter from McMaster University had informed me that I was carefully selected to participate in an on-campus interview for the undergraduate M.D. medical program. The interview package also contained information about an optional pilot activity called the Multiple Mini Interviews (MMIs). At the time, the M.D. program's formal interview day consisted of three activities: watching a video followed by a written essay response, participating in an observed group activity and finally the dreaded panel interview.

Using multiple mini interviews in the medical school admissions' process was unheard of at the time and the concept of multiple mini interviews replacing traditional interviews was still in its infancy. The idea of staying behind after an already long interview day to be a guinea pig was not very enticing but I decided to be a good sport about it. Looking back, the opportunity to participate in the pilot MMIs at McMaster University, prior to their current widespread use worldwide has allowed me to gain a unique perspective on their initial development as an assessment tool and how they continue to shape the admissions' process to medical schools around the globe.

2: Mmi .... Mmu .... Mmwhy?

A common learning approach in medicine has been to *"See one. Do one. Teach one"*. However, when it comes to interviewing for medical school, applicants are often given advice to *"just be themselves"* and left in the dark with respect to interview preparation. Picture yourself among a sea of qualified applicants with stellar GPAs and MCAT scores. Ask yourself the following question truthfully.

Can you realistically distinguish yourself from other highly qualified applicants simply by being yourself?

Medical school admissions' committees are fully aware that the interview is potentially the biggest game changer for any qualified applicant and this is the fundamental reason **why the MMIs came into existence.** In addition to academic achievement, medical schools value an unbiased admission's process that can select for applicants with strong interpersonal skills, integrity and professionalism [1].

Recognizing that traditional interviews are subject to context and evaluator bias, the MMIs were adapted from the objective structured clinical examination (OSCE) to try and minimize interview bias [2]. The rationale for MMIs is that compared with traditional interviews, testing an array of domains of competency, each with a different interviewer, avoids bias attributable to context specificity [3].

As a previous assessor of the MMIs at McMaster University, I continue to see their widespread acceptance and implementation by many health programs. From their inception into the McMaster University medical program's admissions process to widespread use worldwide, the MMIs have been subject to much scrutiny and validation. However, a recent systematic review confirms that MMIs are reliable and statistically predictive of subsequent performance at national medical licensing exams [4]. I believe their use in the admissions' selection process will only continue to grow.

References

1. Eva KW, et. al. An Admissions OSCE: The multiple mini interview. *Medical Education* 2004; 38: 314–326

2. Cameron AJ, et al. Development and Pilot Testing of a Multiple Mini-Interview for Admission to a Pharmacy Degree Program. *Am J Pharm Educ.* 2012 February 10; 76(1): 10.

3. Eva KW, et al. The ability of the multiple mini interview to predict preclerkship performance in medical school. *Acad Med.* 2004;79(10 Suppl):S40–S42.

4. Eva KW, et. al. Association between a medical school admission process using the multiple mini-interview and national licensing examination scores. *JAMA.* 2012 Dec 5;308(21):2233-40

3: Memoir with Dr. MMI

Early on during my third year of residency in Radiation Oncology, I was assigned to rotate with Dr. Harold Reiter, a staff radiation oncologist at Hamilton Health Sciences, McMaster University in Ontario, Canada. In addition to practicing radiation oncology, Dr. Reiter is recognized along with Dr. Kevin Eva and the team at McMaster University for bringing the concept of the MMIs to the admission process in medicine. Given my interest in education, this seemed like the perfect match.

However, the learning environment of the rotation quickly caused my excitement to spiral into a black hole. I was never a fan of "pimping" or being "pimped". Unfortunately, my rotation with Dr. MMI was not a fruitful learning experience and I counted down the days until the start of my next rotation. In medicine, "pimping" is abundant but in my opinion, the institutionalized nature of "pimping" does not absolve the word of its offensive and unethical practice.

I share this personal experience to illustrate an important philosophy. **It is far more effective to teach someone what you know instead of quizzing them on what they don't know.** This is the approach I have taken in consulting many successful applicants and in writing this book.

4: Backbone of an MMI Circuit

Depending on the specific program where you interview, your MMI circuit will likely consist of 6 to 12 stations and may include rest stations. There will be as many participants in your interview circuit as there are stations.

The instructions for each station are typically posted directly outside of each room and you are given up to two minutes to carefully read the prompt prior to entering the room. At the end of the two minutes, a bell will sound and this is your queue to enter the room. Typically, a bell ringer type method is used to keep track of the time and you will be allocated six to eight minutes for each station before moving on to the next station.

During each station, you are expected to complete a task and for most stations, the interviewer will have a standardized set of probing questions to engage you in further discussion. Some programs will provide you with scrap paper to write down your thoughts but the vast majority will not. My suggestion is **to work through your interview preparation with the assumption that you will *not* be able to take notes.**

The types of stations you'll encounter on interview day can essentially be grouped into one of the following categories:

1) Ethical Stations
2) Cultural Competency Stations

3) Social Issues/Health Policy Stations
4) Role Playing Stations
5) Collaboration Stations
6) Traditional Interview Stations
7) Writing Stations
8) Video Stations
9) Rest Stations

Let's explore each category in more detail.

Ethical stations will typically describe a common scenario whereby a fundamental ethical principle is at risk or has been violated and require you to identify and discuss important issues around that ethical principle as it applies to that scenario. The fundamental ethical principles are beneficence, do no harm, justice, autonomy and futility.

Cultural Competency stations typically assess your ability to recognize the cultural characteristics deemed important in order to successfully practice medicine in the school's geographic environment. They typically describe a cultural scenario and require you to identify the controversy and explore the pertinent issues. Examples include gay marriage, gay adoption and legalization of marijuana.

Social Issues & Health Policy stations typically assess your ability to recognize common barriers to the practice of medicine as relevant to the school's geographic environment. They typically include scenarios such as limited access to care in rural health or increased wait times to see a specialist and require you to identify and discuss your approach to handling these issues.

Role Playing stations often involve an actor or standardized patient. You are asked to complete a common task such as delivering bad news, confronting a person about a problem or gathering information from the individual. The interviewer will act as an observer present in the room to assess your language, demeanor and effectiveness at completing the task.

Collaboration stations often require working directly with another co-applicant to complete a task. One applicant provides the instructions while the other receives them. You may be blinded to each other. The scenario can involve a drawing, a series of images or a phone conversation. You are required to complete a given task using only verbal communication and your interaction will be assessed by an interviewer in the room.

Traditional Interview stations are designed to gain insight into who you are and your motivations for selecting a specific health profession and the particular school you are interviewing for. They typically require you to answer one or more questions such as "Why medicine? Why did you apply to this medical school? What are your weaknesses? etc."

Essay writing stations require you to articulate your thoughts on paper within a restricted time interval. These stations are rare and when they do appear are usually 15-20 minutes in length. In general, these stations do not require any verbal communication input. We will not explore essay writing stations any further in this book.

Video stations require you to watch a short clip often less than 40 seconds. The video often highlights a type of relationship and revolves around a conflict. You will not be able to replay the clip so pay close attention. Afterwards, you are required to articulate pertinent details of the interaction to your interviewer succinctly and engage in standardized probing questions. This is the other category that we will not explore any further in this book.

Rest stations allow you the opportunity to refresh and clear your mind. The interview circuit is fast paced and requires a lot of concentration and energy. Since you are not allowed to leave the circuit, you cannot use the rest station as a bathroom break. However, refresher beverages are usually present at rest stations. Use the opportunity to clear your mind and to get ready for the next station instead of dwelling on previous stations.

The nine categories may seem overwhelming as you prepare for your MMIs because in theory they allow for an endless combination of stations. However, in reality there are only **a finite number of personal characteristics assessed.** It is crucial that you remember this fact.

5: The Yes and No of MMIs

In this chapter, we'll focus on what the MMIs assess (the Yes) and what the MMIs don't assess (the No). Applicants to medical, dental, pharmacy, veterinary schools etc. come in all shapes and sizes with a huge variety of background experiences. *Most schools are not interested in further assessing your academic background at the interview stage using the MMIs.* This is an important fact worth remembering and reinforces that the MMIs are used to assess personal characteristics. We'll start off with what the MMIs do not assess. The MMIs:

1. *Do not evaluate any subject based knowledge.* This means that whether you major in music or chemistry, your specific knowledge base in a particular subject will not be tested.

2. *Do not evaluate any clinical based knowledge.* This means that someone who is a nurse will not have an unfair advantage over someone who is a lawyer. Clinical knowledge includes but is not limited to things such as examining, diagnosing or counseling patients on specific medical conditions.

3. *Do not seek a single "right" answer.* This means that there may be many wrong answers but there often isn't a

single acceptable answer. You've likely heard of the euphemism, *"there's more than one way to skin a cat."* The same applies to the MMIs.

Now let's move on to what the MMIs do assess. The MMIs:

1. *Do evaluate your ability to communicate effectively and efficiently in the time allocated.* This is pretty self-explanatory!

2. *Do evaluate your ability to apply general working knowledge to issues relevant to the culture/society in which you live.* This means that the MMIs will evaluate how well you can apply common working knowledge in your decision making process. Although not *explicitly* assessed, one of the key challenges is to learn how to make yourself memorable to the interviewer. Strategies for doing so will be discussed in subsequent chapters as we tackle specific examples.

3. *Do evaluate your ability to think on the spot.* This means that the interviewer is assessing your ability to respond and think critically to different scenarios. Thinking on the spot is often thought to be an innate skill, but like any skill, the secret is to learn how to make the mind more comfortable with the task by establishing a prepared framework to

build your thoughts around. Once your mind is comfortable with the structure, it's easy to fill in the gaps. Fortunately with the MMIs, there are only a finite number of characteristics being assessed.

4. ***Do evaluate and challenge you to defend/discuss your personal opinions.*** As a physician, dentist, pharmacist, veterinarian etc. you will constantly be challenged about your choices and the process behind making those decisions. The MMIs will try to simulate this so it is important to have an opinion, stick to your guns and not flip flop or sit on the fence.

6: K.I.S.S. A.S.S. with the 5 Pockets

The MMIs are administered under strict timed conditions which makes time management a very important aspect to master when practicing for your MMIs. Remember that the most effective answer is going to be the one that delivers your **key message within the first two minutes**. Any longer and you have likely added unnecessary complexity and this must be avoided. In the 1960s, the U.S. Navy introduced the idea that most systems work best if they are kept simple rather than made complex; therefore simplicity should be a key goal in design. The same holds true for the MMIs.

To help you **K.I.S.S. A.S.S.** *(Keep It Short, Simple And Subsequently Succeed)* on interview day, I've devised a framework for the MMIs. It consists of five pockets and the goal is to get you to reach into your pockets as often as you need to. Before we talk about the pockets, let's review some interviewing fundamentals.

Treat each multiple mini interview as a very brief separate job interview. Make sure to read each station's prompt and instructions very carefully. Be sure to *knock* prior to entering each room. As an evaluator, if an applicant fails to knock prior to entering the room, this will get noted. Once you set foot into the room, please *wait to be seated*. Do not assume it's acceptable for you to just sit down at the closest available seat. Depending on the interviewer's preference, they may or may not shake your hand. Please let them **make the first move to shake your hand**. Do not be the first one to initiate a handshake.

The interviewer will likely start each station by asking if you've had a chance to read the prompt and if there are any questions. In the past, there were applicants rejected post interview who claimed they did not have sufficient time to read the prompts.

Use the first 15 seconds of your response and briefly summarize the scenario to the interviewer. **Speak concisely** using minimal words and **avoid distractions** as you are giving your answer. *Common distractions include twiddling your fingers, leg shaking, holding objects in your hands or looking at objects in the room while you are speaking.* If you are guilty of any of the above, video tape yourself so you can see yourself in action and make the changes accordingly. Deliver your answer with clarity and calmly to ensure that your response can be properly heard and understood by the interviewer. If you have a naturally soft voice, I suggest **recording your answers** and playing them back to family members or friends to gauge their opinion.

Avoid fillers such as *"like, uhm, eh"* that will take away from your message and avoid using extreme adjectives such as *"always, never, absolutely, right, wrong etc"* which may be viewed as radical and take away from your answer. In medicine, things are rarely black and white. When the time comes to move on to your next station, remember to **leave your chair in the exact position**

you found it at the beginning. End your station by saying *"thank you for your time"* to the interviewer.

Your brain is literally creating new neural pathways, much like the interstate highway system, carrying information from one neuron to the next as you read this book. The neurons clump together and are associated with each other as one thing leads you to think of another thing. The process seems disorderly without a conscious framework. Understanding that you learn by doing things over and over again may seem rather intuitive but it is the approach you should take in learning how to master the MMIs. From now on, approach each MMI scenario you encounter using the following 5 pockets and allow your brain to think in the same framework over and over again.

Pocket 1 Categorize the MMI station into one of the nine options presented in chapter 4. Hybrid stations (stations that fit into one or more categories do exist but are less likely) should be prioritized into the category you are most comfortable with. The question to ask here is *what general type of scenario does this MMI station fit into?*

Pocket 2 Identify and acknowledge the main issue or problem in the MMI station. Regardless of the task instructions, this is a key step to establishing a neural pathway to each MMI station. Identifying and acknowledging the issue or problem raises awareness within your neuronal networks and will help trigger memories and experiences. The question to ask here is *what is the main issue or problem in this MMI station?*

Pocket 3

Identify the main source of the problem/issue in the MMI station. The goal here is to help you pick out the important concept that you are going to be evaluated on in the station. Train yourself to get into the habit of picking out the main source of the problem and it will be much easier to spot the concept that is being tested. The question to ask here is *what is the main source of the issue or problem in this MMI station?*

Pocket 4

Identify any relevant personal experiences you have that can be incorporated into the MMI station. The goal is for you to leave the most positive lasting impression on the interviewer compared to other applicants on your interview circuit. A very effective method of doing so is by using your personal experiences to sell and set yourself apart from the competition. However, please keep in mind that incorporating personal experiences may not be relevant for certain types of MMI stations such as role playing. I will illustrate with examples as we work through sample MMI stations.

The next chapter is devoted to evaluations but for the time being, keep in mind at some schools, an interviewer must give each applicant a different score. This means that someone is going to get a 1 and someone is going to get a 10. The question to ask here when applicable is *what personal experiences can I include in my answer to make me the most memorable interviewee for this MMI station?*

Pocket 5 Identify ways to resolve or address the problem/issue in the MMI station. At this point, you should get into the habit of exploring the main source of the problem or issue from different viewpoints or perspectives. As you do this, it is important to note in your mind the pros and cons of each perspective. In order to effectively arrive at your answer, you may need to make assumptions. This is absolutely acceptable for the MMIs as long as you are transparent and state your assumptions to the interviewer. If used properly, assumptions will highlight to the interviewer your thought process. The question to ask in this last pocket is *how would I resolve the problem or issue, taking into account my perspective and other perspectives for this MMI station?*

Now that you have your pockets, remember to practice and reach into them often. Let's move on and discuss how the MMIs are scored. Afterwards, we'll spend the remaining chapters applying the 5 pockets to practice MMI scenarios.

7: Scoring the MMIs

General Interviewee tips about MMI Scoring

> ➤ Scores are generally assigned from 0-10.

> ➤ You can score poorly on two stations and still receive an outright admissions offer so don't dwell on your performance in past stations and let it affect your performance on future stations.

> ➤ Many programs drop your highest station and lowest station scores.

> ➤ Remember *ASS* in your evaluations. *A*bility to communicate effectively, *S*trength of arguments and *S*uitability for the program.

General Interviewer Guidelines

Each applicant will have **two** minutes to read the scenario prompt. No more than two minutes should be allocated to read the prompt. At the end of the two minutes, the applicant should be given a minimum of **six** minutes to a maximum of **eight** minutes to complete the task identified in the scenario. Start the interview by asking them *"if they have had a chance to read the entire prompt?"* Do not interrupt the applicant while they are speaking. When they are finished giving their answer, please proceed with the probing questions. At the end of the station, complete the attached evaluation sheets and remember to assign each score only once for each category.

Sample MMI Scoring Template

Please rate the applicant's *overall performance* on this station *relative* to all applicants you are rating. Do not assign a score more than once (ie. if assessing 10 applicants, you may only use a score of 10 once). You may adjust your scores before submitting.

Consider the applicant's:
Ability to communicate effectively
Strength of the arguments displayed
Suitability for the program

Please place an "X" in the desired box below:

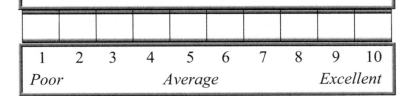

1	2	3	4	5	6	7	8	9	10
Poor				*Average*					*Excellent*

Comments

Part 2
Practice MMI Scenarios

8: MRI Waiting Game

The current average outpatient wait time in your area for an MRI scan is 120 days.

This extended waiting period has sparked a growing concern from the general public who deems this wait time to be unacceptable.

You are hired as a consultant to examine the current situation and make recommendations.

Please discuss your recommendation(s) with the interviewer.

Pocket 1 *What general type of scenario does this MMI station fit into?*

Pocket 2 *What is the main problem or issue in this MMI station?*

Pocket 3 *What is the main source of the problem or issue in this MMI station?*

Pocket 4 *What personal experience do I have to include that is relevant to this MMI station?*

Pocket 5 *How would I resolve the problem or issue, taking into account my perspective and other perspectives for this MMI station?*

Answers to Pocket Questions

Pocket 1: Health policy category.
Pocket 2: Wait times which are unacceptable.
Pocket 3: Lack of resources or resource allocation.

At this point you should be drawing together pockets 1- 4 to formulate your recommendations. In pocket 3, we identify that the source of the problem is potentially the lack of resources or resource allocation. Examples of lack of resources would include inadequate number of MRI machines, inadequate facilities to house MRI machines and inadequate number of properly trained personnel to operate MRI machines. Examples of resource allocation considerations would include parameters around how the MRI machines are used such as number of hours or days per week the machines are operated, the number of MRI scans being ordered by each provider, and the cost of educating the public and health force on proper utilization of MRI scans.

You should jot down your opinion for each of the above examples and possible solutions to the above considerations. As you come up with your recommendations, in the back of your mind, be prepared to defend why your recommendations should be accepted.

What is resource allocation?

Resource allocation is the distribution of goods and services to programs and people. In the context of healthcare, macroallocations of resources are made by governments at the national, provincial/state and municipal levels [1]. Mesoallocations are made at the level of institutions and microallocations are made at the level of the individual patient [1].

Why is resource allocation important?

As public and professional expectations continue to increase, costly new technologies must be balanced against tightly monitored health care budgets, competing government priorities and provincial deficits [1].

Sample Model Response

Interviewer: "Please discuss your recommendations for this scenario."

Applicant: "This is a scenario where the public has grown concerned about the lengthy wait times to obtain an outpatient MRI scan. I recognize that this is a complex situation and after carefully exploring the issues of resource allocation and lack of resources, my recommendations would be to implement a provider tracking system to better understand how MRI appointments are being filled by physicians and to make changes to the way the MRI machines are currently being operated. In helping me arrive at my recommendations, I've found that the lengthy wait times were contributed by factors such as inappropriate MRI machine operating hours, as well as MRI scans being ordered for inpatients when they weren't indicated which further lengthened the wait times for outpatient MRI scans."

Probing Questions

✓ What other factors did you consider in making your recommendations?

✓ What will you do if the wait times don't improve 1 year after your recommendations are adopted?

✓ Where do you see the role of patient education fitting into this scenario?

✓ Is there anything else you'd like to mention that has not yet been covered?

References

1. McKneally MF, et al. Bioethics for clinicians: 13. Resource allocation. *Can Med Assoc J* 1997;157:163-7

9: *Finding Out You Have Cancer*

You are a primary care provider. Mr. Reed is a 52 year old male whom you saw four weeks ago in your outpatient clinic. It has been two weeks since he underwent a prostate biopsy. Unfortunately the results of his prostate biopsy confirm a cancer diagnosis.

He is here to find out the results of his biopsy. Upon arrival Mr. Reed is placed in an examining room by your nurse who subsequently informs you that he appears very anxious.

Please enter the examining room and interact with Mr. Reed. During your encounter please discuss the results of his biopsy with him.

Pocket 1 | *What general type of scenario does this MMI station fit into?*

Pocket 2 | *What is the main problem or issue in this MMI station?*

Pocket 3 | *What is the main source of the problem or issue in this MMI station?*

Pocket 4 | *What personal experience do I have to include that is relevant to this MMI station?*

Pocket 5 | *How would I resolve the problem or issue, taking into account my perspective and other perspectives for this MMI station?*

Answers to Pocket Questions

Pocket 1: Role Play/Acting.
Pocket 2: How to effectively deliver bad news.
Pocket 3: New prostate cancer diagnosis.

As you start to mentally plan your upcoming encounter with Mr. Reed, remember that the interviewer in the room is not going to evaluate your knowledge of any aspects surrounding "prostate" cancer. However, making incorrect statements about prostate cancer treatment decisions or providing "advice" on prostate cancer will work against you and take away from your main goal of effectively delivering bad news.

Interviewees frequently cite role playing stations as being one of the most challenging categories because of their artificial settings and the their unpredictable paths. You can't change the settings of these stations but with a few tricks we'll go over, I'll show you how you can always take control of these scenarios and keep the ball in your court.

What is bad news?

Quite simply, bad news may be defined as "any information which adversely and seriously affects an individual's view of his or her future" [1]. Delivering bad news is complex and in addition to the verbal component of disclosing bad news, it also includes responding to patients' emotional reactions, involving the patient in decision-making, dealing with the stress created by patients' expectations for cure, the involvement of multiple family members, and the dilemma of how to give hope when the situation is bleak [2].

Why is delivering bad news important?

How bad news is disseminated to patients' will affect their level of comprehension, their level of hopefulness, subsequent psychological adjustment and ultimately their satisfaction with medical care received [3].

The effects of bad news on an individual's well-being are life changing. The process is stressful for both the provider and recipient. Research suggests that physicians who are comfortable in delivering bad news may be subject to less stress and burnout [4]. If you already have an approach to delivering bad news, follow along and see how yours compares.

Start by taking a thorough look around at your environment. Make a mental note of the room setting (ie. quiet, noisy, private) and assess for accessories in the room (ie. tissue box, table, chair arrangements). *Ask yourself if the setting is appropriate for delivering bad news?*

It is important to have clear comprehension of what the individual already understands and the breadth of information they would like to know before diving in with any bad news. A simple question to tease this information out is to ask, *"Are you the type of person that wants to know all the little details or do you prefer to have the big picture?*

If they are unaccompanied, make sure to address whether there is anyone else they'd like to have present for the discussion. Remember to pause after delivering bad news. Acknowledge emotions shown and let the individual know that *"we will continue when they are ready"*. Make sure you have a clear understanding in your mind of what they need at this point prior to ending your discussion.

Sample Model Response

Applicant: Enters room after knocking, greets Mr. Reed by shaking his hand and introduces themselves properly. *"Hello Mr. Reed. Welcome back. Thank you for coming in today."*

Mr. Reed: "Thanks Doc."

Applicant: "Mr. Reed. Do you remember why we did that biopsy on your prostate several weeks ago?"

Mr. Reed: "Well, you said my prostate felt enlarged on physical exam and I was having trouble going to the bathroom."

Applicant: "That's right. We were hoping the biopsy would give us a better understanding of why your prostate is enlarged and it has. However before we talk about that in more detail, how have you been since your biopsy?"

Mr. Reed: "Unfortunately, very anxious."

Applicant: "You do look anxious. Is it because of the biopsy or because of something else?"

Mr. Reed: "Not knowing the results of the biopsy and fearing that I might have cancer are the main reasons why I'm anxious doc."

Applicant: "I understand. You mentioned cancer. Can you remind me whether you know anyone with cancer?

Mr. Reed: "Yes, but they have all passed."

Applicant: "I'm sorry to hear that Mr. Reed. I know it must be difficult for you to talk about this. I want to focus a bit more on you. In general, are you the type of person who likes to know all the details or do you prefer the big picture?"

Mr. Reed: "Big picture doc."

Applicant: "That's helpful for me to know. Did you come here by yourself today?"

Mr. Reed: "My brother is in the waiting room."

Interviewee: "Would you like me to bring him in for our discussion or is there anyone else you'd like to have present?"

Mr. Reed: "That's ok doc. Thanks for asking."

Applicant: "Mr. Reed, I know that you mentioned you are anxious because the thought of having "cancer" is in the back of your mind. The prostate biopsy that was done several weeks ago does show cancer cells in the prostate. (Pause)

Mr. Reed: "So I have cancer doc?" (Starts to become emotional)

Applicant: (Hands tissue box to patient) *"I know this is life changing information but the biopsy results do show cancel cells in the prostate, Mr. Reed."*

Mr. Reed: *"I'm sorry, I don't usually cry. So am I going to die doc?"*

Applicant: "I know a lot must be going through your mind right now. Before we talk about anything else, can you please tell me what you need from me right now?

Mr. Reed: *"I don't know. Can we talk about my treatment?"*

Applicant: "For the time being, I have just given you life changing information. I want to better understand what I can do right now to support you."

Mr. Reed: *"I'm not sure doc. I think I just need some time right now to let it all sink in."*

Applicant: "I understand. Would you like me to bring you back next week after you've had some time to let things sink in?

Mr. Reed: *"yes, thanks doc."*

Applicant: "In the meantime, if there's something you need to talk about, please call my office. I will see you soon Mr. Reed. Please don't feel rushed and take your time leaving." (Shakes hand with Mr. Reed before leaving room)

What can you say in role playing scenarios when you know you've gone down the wrong path?

This scenario would have likely taken several turns for the worse if the interviewee had fallen for Mr. Reed's traps by answering his questions on treatment options and whether he'll succumb from his cancer. Remember that you are not being evaluated on your knowledge base in a particular subject. In this case, it is impossible to make sound treatment recommendations based on the information given in the scenario.

However, if you started talking about radiation therapy, chemotherapy or surgery for Mr. Reed without knowing important prognostic factors for prostate cancer such as the PSA level or Gleason score, then it's important to have a get out of jail strategy in your back pocket. One key phrase that works well in most role playing scenarios is, *"Before I go into any more details about treatment options, can you please tell me what's going through your mind?"* If you get challenged and the individual insists that you continue down the same path regarding something you have no clue about, then just stand your ground and say, *"I hear what you are saying (Mr. Reed) and we will talk about your treatment but right now, I'm more worried about how this life changing information is affecting you. Is it ok if we spend a bit more time exploring this?"*

Remember, the MMIs are very much about showing you have control and being able to take on the heat without sweating!

References

1. Buckman R. Breaking Bad News: A Guide for Health Care Professionals. Baltimore: *Johns Hopkins University Press*, 1992:15.

2. Baile WF, et al. SPIKES—A Six-Step Protocol for Delivering Bad News: Application to the Patient with Cancer. *The Oncologist* 2000, 5:302-311

3. Butow PN, et al. Communication with cancer patients: does it matter? *J Palliat Care* 1995;11:34-38.

4. Ramirez AJ et al. Burnout and psychiatric disorder among cancer clinicians. *Br J Cancer* 1995;71:1263-1269

10: *Group Work Blues*

Each week you gather with your tutorial group to review material assigned to each team member from the previous week. The work is divided up among your group equally such that each team member is responsible for learning a specific aspect of the material and then reporting back to the rest of the group.

You consistently feel frustrated with one member of the group who repeatedly comes to the group sessions late and unprepared.

Please discuss with the interviewer what you would do in this situation and be prepared to justify your response.

Pocket 1 — *What general type of scenario does this MMI station fit into?*

Pocket 2 — *What is the main problem or issue in this MMI station?*

Pocket 3 — *What is the main source of the problem or issue in this MMI station?*

Pocket 4 — *What personal experience do I have to include that is relevant to this MMI station?*

Pocket 5 — *How would I resolve the problem or issue, taking into account my perspective and other perspectives for this MMI station?*

Answers to Pocket Questions

Pocket 1: Traditional Interview category
(Self-Reflection/Conflict Management)
Pocket 2: Conflict among group work.
Pocket 3: Perceived lack of co-operation among a
team member.

This MMI station touches upon several themes including conflict management, group work and self-reflection. Interviewees frequently have no difficulty identifying the underlying conflict and group work themes of the scenario. However, self-reflection is also central to the scenario and is more often missed by interviewees.

What is Self Reflection?

Self-reflection is the active conscious process of placing emphasis and thought into one's character, actions and motives. Combining self-reflection with structured learning is a useful tool for helping students increase self-awareness and ease anxiety that may interfere with learning [1].

General approach to group work situations

Before we can address any potential group dynamics that exist among the team, the interviewee has to first rule out any potential personal sources of bias that may exist. If there are potential biases, make sure to acknowledge and address those first.

Disagreements inevitably arise among group work. To remain cohesive as one unit, any potential concerns should first be brought up to the remaining group members minus the individual(s) whom concerns have been identified. We have all heard casual statements from individuals claiming that *"for any MMI station there is no such thing as a wrong answer."* **From my experience, having been in involved on both sides of the admissions' process, there are clearly wrong answers for _EVERY_ MMI station.** An incorrect approach in this situation would be to directly confront this team member immediately about their tardiness and lack of preparedness without first speaking to the other group members.

After first speaking with the group and establishing group consensus, the next step should be to identify how to bring up the issue(s) with the individual of concern. During the discussion, make sure to address both your concerns, the group's concerns and any personal concerns raised by the individual of concern. At this point offer them support when appropriate. In pocket 3, we identified the perceived lack of cooperation among this team member as being the source of the problem (arriving late and being unprepared were two sources of frustration mentioned in the prompt). In your mind, explore possible reasons to account for this individual arriving late and unprepared.

Most of us have been in a situation involving a group conflict at some point so use these scenarios as opportunities for you to share your own personal experience with your interviewer. We won't get into the specifics in this book about how to present your personal experiences but this is something I routinely do one on one with my applicants during our mock interview sessions. As you come up with your answer about what you would do in this situation, in the back of your mind, be prepared to justify why.

Sample Model Response

Interviewer: "Can you please tell me what you would do in this situation?"

Applicant: "This is a scenario where I'm a member of a weekly tutorial group and one of my classmates repeatedly comes to the sessions late and unprepared. I would first take a step back and ask myself if I might have any personal bias towards this group member that could be contributing to my feelings of frustration. Afterwards, I would meet with my group (without this individual present) and see if other members had any concerns about this individual before sharing mine. Assuming we are all on the same page, I would offer suggestions on how to proceed and ask for group feedback. I was involved in a similar group work situation in my undergrad history course and we were able to move forward by exploring the potential reasons why our team member was unprepared and late for our sessions. Once I knew the reasons, I was able to offer support to help them. Having been through a similar experience, I wouldn't want to confront this individual on my own without first undergoing self-reflection and making sure I had the support of my group."

Probing Questions

✓ Why should the other group members accept your suggestions?

✓ What will you do if things continue to persist with this same individual?

✓ What are some potential consequences of directly confronting this individual?

✓ Is there any role for reporting this individual's behavior to higher authority?

✓ Do you prefer to learn in groups or on your own?

Common pitfalls to avoid

As you carefully read the MMI station prompt, pay close attention to the wording and gender descriptors. Notice that in this MMI scenario, wording was carefully chosen such to not reveal the sex of the team member in question. This is done deliberately in an attempt to catch you off guard and have you put your foot in your mouth. I've work͏ with many applicants during mock MMI interv͏ sessions and a recurring pitfall is that appli͏ tend to associate behaviors such as lack of coop with male gender and roles such as nursing with female gender. It's amazing how many times I've heard applicants assume the group member in this scenario is "a guy" and referred to them as "him" in their answer. **Remember to be as gender neutral as the prompt you're reading.**

Another pitfall in this situation is to forget that you are working in a group and directly confront this individual without first seeking group input. Your approach to group work situations should be to resolve issues as a cohesive functional unit rather than as an overly confident and aggressive team member.

References

1. Ganzer CA, et al. Structured learning and self-reflection: strategies to decrease anxiety in the psychiatric mental health clinical nursing experience. *Nurs Educ Perspect.* 2013 Jul-Aug;34(4):244-7.

Please discuss with the interviewer your decision to pursue a career as a physician.

In your answer, please include any relevant factor(s) that lead to your decision to apply to medical school.

Pocket 1 — *What general type of scenario does this MMI station fit into?*

Pocket 2 — *What is the main problem or issue in this MMI station?*

Pocket 3 — *What is the main source of the problem or issue in this MMI station?*

Pocket 4 — *What personal experience do I have to include that is relevant to this MMI station?*

Pocket 5 — *How would I resolve the problem or issue, taking into account my perspective and other perspectives for this MMI station?*

Answers to Pocket Questions

Pocket 1: Traditional Interview category
(Why Medicine)
Pocket 2: Discussing why you want to be a doctor.
Pocket 3: Effectively being able to sell your story about why medicine to the interviewer.

In this MMI station, your perspective refers to your unique story for entering medicine and other perspectives refers to your thoughts for deciding against entering other health professions. A strong, credible answer to this MMI station will allow the interviewer to clearly remember you from other interviewees. Your personal story if told correctly will make it obvious to the interviewer that you have placed significant emphasis and have undergone significant relevant experiences to adequately prepare yourself for a future career in medicine.

Why medicine and not another health profession?

Doctors interact daily with other health care professionals in multidisciplinary settings. The role of each health care professional is important in providing efficient, patient centered care. Physicians have largely shifted away from the captain of the ship model to a much more team based approach.

Therefore, *it is just as important for you to be able to justify why other health care professions are not the best fit as it is for you to be able to confidently tell your interviewer why you want to go into medicine.* To help you formulate your answer, please keep in mind the ways medicine differs from other health professions and ask yourself *how are these differences able to better account for my fit in a career?*

General approach to Why Medicine ..

Even though "why medicine" is a highly personalized answer, a few general comments can be said about the components of a "strong" answer.

> ➤ A strong answer clearly identifies that the applicant has thought about other health care professions and has ultimately arrived at the conclusion that being a physician is the career that best suits them.

> ➤ A strong answer clearly shows that the applicant understands what the profession of medicine has to offer them and forms a strong bridge with their past experiences.

> ➤ A strong answer clearly portrays the applicant's interest in being a physician chronologically in such a way that shows adequate preparation for a career in medicine.

Sample Model Response

Interviewer: "Can you please tell me about your decision to pursue a career as a doctor."

Applicant: "My decision to apply to medical school to become a doctor is the result of all of my experiences. After learning about diseases in my undergraduate biology course, I began to think about health care as a career option and I wanted to explore this further. Over the years, I've sought out experiences in different health professions and enjoyed them to a certain degree but the field that is most satisfying and the best fit for me is medicine. Being able to help people is not enough for me. I want a career that will allow me the flexibility to take care of people, be an educator and also conduct research. In terms of taking care of people, I really value the unique patient-doctor relationship I've observed in my volunteer work. I've also participated in medical research in my undergrad and this non-clinical aspect of medicine was very rewarding for me. These are just a few of the experiences I've sought out which have helped further solidify my decision to apply to medical school and become a physician."

Probing Questions

✓ What will you do if you don't get into medical school this year?

✓ What do you think is the most challenging aspect to being a physician?

✓ What do you think is the most rewarding aspect to being a physician?

✓ What do you think is the least rewarding aspect to being a physician?

12: Bury or Scatter?

The belief held by many Aboriginals is that they come from the land. This plays a great deal of importance in discussing ceremonies about death.

You are a funeral home manager looking after funeral arrangements for Mr. Acorn; a 55 yo Aboriginal who passed unexpectedly from a heart attack two days ago. He has not left behind any advanced directives.

His wife of 33 years strongly believes he should be buried whereas his parents strongly oppose a burial and believe he should be cremated with his ashes scattered over the land. You cannot proceed any further with Mr. Acorn's funeral arrangements until a decision is made regarding the type of burial.

Please discuss with the interviewer how you would handle this situation.

| Pocket 1 | *What general type of scenario does this MMI station fit into?* |

| Pocket 2 | *What is the main problem or issue in this MMI station?* |

| Pocket 3 | *What is the main source of the problem or issue in this MMI station?* |

| Pocket 4 | *What personal experience do I have to include that is relevant to this MMI station?* |

| Pocket 5 | *How would I resolve the problem or issue, taking into account my perspective and other perspectives for this MMI station?* |

Answers to Pocket Questions

> Pocket 1: Cultural Competency category (can also consider as Ethical category)
> Pocket 2: Conflict among the patient's spouse and family belief systems.
> Pocket 3: Lack of written advanced directives provided by the patient.

This MMI station highlights real world challenges that can happen when a loved one dies unexpectedly without having established a clear set of advanced directives. The situation is further complicated by Mr. Acorn's parents who hold a different belief system than Mr. Acorn's wife. In coming up with your own answer to this scenario, please remember that our ultimate goal in this case is to make the best possible decision by carrying out Mr. Acorn's final wishes.

The basis of Aboriginal beliefs

Aboriginal beliefs are rooted in the context of oral history and culture. For Aboriginal people, decision-making is best understood as a process and not as the correct interpretation of a unified code [1]. Mr. Acorn's parents were likely raised in a belief system that emphasizes achieving balance and wellness within the domains of human life (mental, physical, emotional and spiritual). The process of spreading his ashes over the land likely represents this balance symbolically.

Substitute Decision Making

On the other hand, Mr. Acorn's wife of 33 years seems to believe that her husband should be buried. In any situation where the patient is not able to advocate for themselves, a substitute decision maker should be carefully selected. The substitute decision-maker should be the person or persons with the best knowledge of the patient's specific wishes, the patient's values and beliefs and should have the patient's best interests at heart [2]. Keep in mind the difference between values, beliefs and wishes. The patient's wishes are those preferences expressed by the patient that are relevant to the decision that needs to be made.

On the other hand, values and beliefs are generally less specific than wishes but allow the substitute decision-maker to infer, in light of other choices the patient has made (ie their approach to life), what they would decide in the present situation. When family members disagree on which course of action to take, they should be encouraged to focus their attention towards what the patient would have wanted. The criteria on which the decision should be based on are [2]:

1. The patient's previously explicitly stated wishes.
2. The patient's known values and beliefs.
3. The patient's best interests.

What is the role of the health care professional in Substitute Decision Making?

Simply stated, the health care professional's role here is to facilitate the process of substitute decision-making by providing information that will result in an informed choice on the patient's behalf. Health care professionals act as chaperones in the process and help guide the substitute(s) to consider the patient's previously expressed wishes, their values and beliefs, and their best interests [2].

Sample Model Response

Interviewer: *"Can you please tell me how you would handle this situation?"*

Applicant: "As the funeral home manager, this is a scenario where there is disagreement between family members regarding the proper end of life burial procedures. Mr. Acorn has not left behind any advanced directives and while his wife believes that her husband should be buried, Mr. Acorn's parents believe that their son should be cremated. Unfortunately, this illustrates the complexities that arise when no previously substitute decision maker or advanced directives are in place. I would have a thorough discussion individually with both his wife and his parents about Mr. Acorn's belief system. I would also speak with anyone else that may have played a significant part in his life such as close friends or children. After having gathered these pieces of the puzzle, I would share my findings with his parents and his wife in the hopes of coming to a mutual agreement on how to proceed in the best interests of Mr. Acorn.

Probing Questions

- ✓ What would you do next if there was still no agreement on Mr. Acorn's burial procedures?

- ✓ What values and beliefs are most important in guiding your decision in this scenario?

- ✓ Who do you ultimately feel should have the final say in this scenario?

- ✓ Are there other individuals you would enlist the help of?

References

1. Ellerby JH, et al. Bioethics for clinicians: 18. Aboriginal cultures. *CMAJ* October 3, 2000 vol. 163 no. 7.

2. Lazar NM, et al. Bioethics for clinicians: 5: Substitute Decision Making. *CMAJ* 1996; 155: 1435-1437

13: A Medication Overdose

You are a pharmacy student doing a clinical rotation on the surgical floor at a community hospital. It is early in the morning and after rounding, the surgical team members have departed for the operating room. You are about to go into a room to speak with Ms. Carol about her diabetes medication when her shift nurse pulls you aside and informs you she gave Ms. Carol 5 times the regular ordered dose of her blood pressure medication 20 minutes ago. The nurse has tried to page the surgery team twice but has been unsuccessful. No prescribed changes were made to Ms. Carol's medication record over the past 24 hours. You are the first person to be notified of this new information and the nurse tells you that Ms. Carol is currently stable and comfortable.

Please discuss the course of action you would take with the interviewer. In your answer, please explore the issues pertinent to this scenario.

Pocket 1	*What general type of scenario does this MMI station fit into?*
Pocket 2	*What is the main problem or issue in this MMI station?*
Pocket 3	*What is the main source of the problem or issue in this MMI station?*
Pocket 4	*What personal experience do I have to include that is relevant to this MMI station?*
Pocket 5	*How would I resolve the problem or issue, taking into account my perspective and other perspectives for this MMI station?*

Answers to Pocket Questions

Pocket 1: Ethical category
Pocket 2: Full disclosure and patient safety.
Pocket 3: Medical error involving an overdose of
prescribed drug therapy.

This MMI station highlights that errors are inevitable and real in the health care setting. Medical professionals will face situations where they must address mistakes that have been made with their patients. In most cases, errors are not the result of a single factor such as negligence but rather a complex array of interconnected factors. In this scenario, a medication error is reported to you and the patient remains unaware that they were given five times the prescribed dose of their blood pressure medication.

What is a Medical Error?

Medical errors are usually considered to be preventable adverse medical events and are the result of omission or commission [1].

Important considerations for Medical Errors

The disclosure of a medical error represents a challenging situation for health care providers [2]. Before full disclosure can occur, patient safety must take precedence.

Patient safety is of utmost importance after any committed medical error and must be fully addressed with the most responsible medical team. In more challenging scenarios where the medical error **did not** result in harm, *it should automatically be assumed that the patient would want full disclosure, regardless of the magnitude of the medical error.*

The full disclosure process should follow our guidelines for delivering bad news (see chapter 9) and take place in a private setting when the patient is medically stable and is able to comprehend the discussion.

Lack of trust is a reality after a medical error has been disclosed. Patients often experience a loss of trust in the medical system and the involved health care team members when informed that a mistake has been made [3]. However, with an open dialogue, this loss of trust can be subsequently regained in comparison with the permanent loss of trust that results when a patient confirms that their health care team has not been fully transparent in their care.

As you formulate your answer to our scenario involving Ms. Carol, pay close attention to pocket 3 which requires you to examine the main source of the issue/problem. In this case, a medical error has occurred but digging a little deeper below the surface, one could ask, *why did the nurse give 5x the prescribed dose? Could the nurse have been a new employee and inexperienced? Perhaps this was her first time taking care of this patient and she misread the prescription order in Ms. Carol's chart?* Remember that when it comes to the MMIs, examining for the source of the issue/problem will not require any explicit clinical or subject based knowledge. Instead, use your common background knowledge to prioritize the important considerations I've illustrated. Ultimately ask yourself, *how might this medical error have been prevented and approach it from both the nurse's and the patient's perspectives.*

Sample Model Response

Interviewer: "Can you please discuss the course of action you would take in this situation?"

Applicant: "I'm the first to be notified by Ms. Carol's nurse that a medical error was made resulting in her receiving 5x the prescribed dose of her blood pressure medication. Even though Ms. Carol is currently stable and comfortable, the most pressing issue remains patient safety. She should be carefully monitored for any changes in discomfort or symptoms. I would next address this medical error with full disclosure to my supervisor, the surgical team and to Ms. Carol. By telling the patient that a mistake has been made, this would probably affect her outlook on the quality of care she has received. However, only by being fully honest and accountable do we stand the best chance of regaining her trust. To better understand why a mistake has been made, I would want to speak in more detail with her nurse regarding the exact surrounding circumstances in the hopes that similar errors could be prevented in the future."

Probing Questions

✓ What might you suggest to the nurse to help prevent similar future errors from happening?

✓ Is there a role for reporting the nurse to higher authority?

✓ Who should ultimately be held accountable for this medical error?

✓ Are there circumstances where it would be justified not to fully disclose that a medical error was made to the patient?

References

1. Brennan T. et al. Incidence of adverse events and negligence in hospitalized patients: results of the Harvard Medical Practice Study I. *N Engl J Med* 1991;324:370-6.

2. Hilfiker D. Facing our mistakes. *N Engl J Med* 1984;310:118-22.

3. Diekema DS. ETHICS IN MEDICINE University of Washington School of Medicine. Online. Accessed October 8, 2013

14: Same-Sex Parenting

You are a senior medical student interested in becoming a pediatrician. It is the first day of your outpatient pediatrics elective. The staff pediatrician has asked you to tag along to see David, a 6 year old child brought in by his parents with a cough. Shortly after the encounter, the staff pediatrician tells you they feel sorry for David, as he has two dads. They believe that this is morally unacceptable because it will put David at increased risk for psychiatric disorders such as depression when he gets older. However, there is no scientific evidence to support the pediatrician's belief that children with same sex parents are at increased risk of psychiatric disorders. You feel something must be done about this situation.

Please discuss the course of action you would take with the interviewer.

Pocket 1	*What general type of scenario does this MMI station fit into?*
Pocket 2	*What is the main problem or issue in this MMI station?*
Pocket 3	*What is the main source of the problem or issue in this MMI station?*
Pocket 4	*What personal experience do I have to include that is relevant to this MMI station?*
Pocket 5	*How would I resolve the problem or issue, taking into account my perspective and other perspectives for this MMI station?*

Answers to Pocket Questions

Pocket 1: Cultural Competency category
Pocket 2: Provider bias
Pocket 3: Personal and/or religious beliefs that are
       interfering with patient care.

Both healthcare providers and patients may bring cultural, religious and ideological beliefs with them as they enter into a mutual patient-physician relationship. Occasionally, these beliefs may challenge or conflict with what the physician believes to be medically acceptable [1]. Medical encounters are generally a source of anxiety for the general population. For gay and lesbian patients, such normal stresses are further magnified by concerns related to sexual orientation [2]. In our MMI station, David's parents do not engage in a direct patient-physician relationship with the staff pediatrician but the physician's comments suggest that the patient-physician relationship with David may be negatively affected by their belief system and false perceptions of David's environment. In other words, we are dealing with provider bias.

What is Cultural Competency?

Cultural competency is the ability to interact effectively with people of different cultures and socio-economic backgrounds without bias. The concept of cultural competency has a positive effect on patient care delivery by enabling providers to deliver care that is respectful of and responsive to the health beliefs, practices and cultural and linguistic needs of diverse patients [3].

Important considerations for Cultural Competency

Developing cultural competency is critical to reducing health disparities and improving access to high-quality health care, health care that is respectful of and responsive to the needs of diverse patients [3].

Self-identification by the patient or individual group is a key consideration of cultural competency. This involves using language and dialogue similar to that used by the individual to establish better understanding and rapport.

Advocating for patients is at the heart of cultural competency. In this scenario, David's parents are not aware of their pediatrician's belief system. However, as a medical student working on the rotation, you are privy to this new information and to not advocate for David and his family would be acting like the *"elephant in the room"*.

However, from your perspective as an aspiring pediatrician, confronting your pediatrician staff might be equivalent to committing career suicide and you may be labeled as a trouble maker for stirring the pot. One very important thing I've learned as a doctor is that it is much more difficult to do the right thing rather than to just turn a blind eye. However, at the end of the day, you're going to be the one that has to live with the consequences of your choices. I know that for me, even though it was difficult at the time to do the right thing, looking back, I wouldn't have it any other way. Getting off my soap box, let's get back to the scenario.

One approach for bringing up concerns with a superior is to start with the facts and ask for clarification. With David's case, you could ask for the evidence behind the pediatrician's comments. The main reasons for bringing up concerns with this pediatrician are to advocate for David, his family and improve the overall quality of healthcare. Your goal is not to complain about the past so we're not going to go there. You can use information from the past to inform the situation, but make sure to stay focused on what needs to be done to move forward so that patients are not subjected to provider bias.

Sample Model Response

Interviewer: "Can you please discuss the course of action you would take in this situation?"

Applicant: "This is the first day on my pediatrics elective and I've been told by my staff that the patient we just saw will have a higher chance of developing psychiatric conditions when he gets older because he has two dads. I would ask to speak with my staff in private, seek clarification and supporting evidence behind their comments. My main goal from our discussion is to improve the quality of care provided to David and future patients like David by not subjecting them to provider bias. However, by speaking with my staff, this may negatively affect my chances of become a pediatrician. I was in a similar situation at work where I interacted with my superior about management concerns and despite thinking that it was going to be job suicide, it ended up improving the dynamics of our work environment. Alternatively, by not speaking up, I would be the elephant in the room and for me, that isn't an option."

Probing Questions

- ✓ What are other relevant considerations for this scenario?

- ✓ Is it appropriate and/or necessary to disclose to David's parents the staff pediatrician's beliefs regarding same sex families?

- ✓ What are the challenges to achieving cultural competency?

- ✓ How does provider bias affect patient care?

Common Pitfall to Avoid

How many of you were thinking that this was a male pediatrician? If you answered yes, you're not alone! This is likely because from an early age, we are programmed to believe that women are more accepting and nurturing (and vice versa for men). However, keep in mind that the pediatrician's gender was never disclosed! Once again, remember not to fall for the incorrect gender assumption pitfall!!

References

1. Diekema DS. Cross-cultural Issues and Diverse Beliefs. Ethics in Medicine: University of Washington School of Medicine. Web. Accessed Oct 13th, 2013.

2. Stein GL, et al. Original Research: Physician–Patient Relationships Among the Lesbian and Gay Community. *Journal of the Gay and Lesbian Medical Association* September 2001, Volume 5, Issue 3, pp 87-93

3. NIH Communication: Cultural Competency http://www.nih.gov/clearcommunication/cult uralcompetency.htm accessed Oct 13th, 2013

15: Opps ... I Made a Mistake

You are a family physician with a busy clinic. Your next patient is Mr. Diode, an elderly gentleman who has been under your care for his type II diabetes, asthma and recurring angina. He was last seen by you 5 weeks ago. You quickly review his chart prior to seeing him and to your disappointment you realize that his last electrocardiogram tracing done 6 weeks ago shows an abnormal ST segment elevation. The report was received in your office before Mr. Diode's last visit but you have not seen these results until now.

Please discuss what you would say to Mr. Diode with the interviewer.

Pocket 1 — *What general type of scenario does this MMI station fit into?*

Pocket 2 — *What is the main problem or issue in this MMI station?*

Pocket 3 — *What is the main source of the problem or issue in this MMI station?*

Pocket 4 — *What personal experience do I have to include that is relevant to this MMI station?*

Pocket 5 — *How would I resolve the problem or issue, taking into account my perspective and other perspectives for this MMI station?*

Answers to Pocket Questions

Pocket 1: Ethical category.
Pocket 2: Omission of information.
Pocket 3: EKG results were missed 6 weeks ago and
not disclosed to patient at their last visit.

The first thing you've probably noticed is that the vocabulary used in this MMI scenario is more technical than other examples we've seen. The scenario is filled with medical jargon such as "angina" and "ST segment elevation" which would throw any medical school applicant off. Fortunately, this is the type of MMI station that is likely to be reserved for a postgraduate residency interview (but in theory could appear on any health MMI circuit). There is no denying that it would be helpful to understand that angina means chest pain and to know that the significance of ST segment elevation on an electrocardiogram is that the heart is not receiving enough oxygen.

However, the above medical knowledge is not a prerequisite for performing well on this station as we'll continue to demonstrate using our 5 pockets approach. There is more than enough information provided in laymen's terms in the prompt to allow any applicant to effectively succeed.

The primary objective in this station is honesty and whether an applicant is able to be responsible and accountable for mistakes they may make. Honesty is consistently reported as one of the most important attributes of physicians in the medical education literature and may be the attribute that instills trust at all levels of medical practice [1]. This MMI station falls under the ethical category (Pocket 1) and the main problem is omission of information (Pocket 2). The main source of the problem is that important medical information was not disclosed to the patient five weeks ago by their doctor (Pocket 3). Pocket four deals with any relevant personal experience you have. If you've made it this far, please go ahead and finish pocket 5 on your own before reading any further and comparing your answer with the sample model answer.

Stations with "Difficult Language Syndrome"

The MMIs are designed to be a high stress experience compared to the traditional personal interview. Given the tight time constraints, **there is little to no emphasis on getting to know the applicant on a personal level.** Rather, the MMIs aim to strategically expose your personal qualities and weaknesses through a standardized approach.

It is not uncommon to experience unfamiliar language in an MMI prompt. Difficult Language Syndrome (DLS) refers to the use of *words that are unreasonably beyond the scope of the applicant's vocabulary.* If you find yourself in such a situation, ask yourself *what is the overall big picture in this prompt?* Using our example, the overall big picture minus DLS is that as a physician, you've missed an important result when you saw this patient five weeks ago. You are seeing them now and have the opportunity to move forward with this new information.

Don't fall for those DLS distractors which in this case, will take you away from your ability to focus on the reasons *why* you may have missed this critical information five weeks ago and *how* you can prevent a recurrence.

Sample Model Response

Interviewer: "Can you please discuss what you would say to Mr. Diode in this situation?"

Applicant: "I'm seeing Mr. Diode for a 5 week follow up visit and after reviewing his chart I notice that he had an EKG test 6 weeks ago which shows an abnormality. However, this is my first time being aware of these results. I would begin by asking how he is doing and if there have been any changes since we last met. Assuming no changes have taken place since our last encounter, I would start a conversation regarding the missed EKG result. I would notify him that he had an EKG test done 6 weeks ago and the results were mailed to my attention shortly thereafter but I did not see them until today. After acknowledging and being honest about my mistake, I'll let him know that I'm in the process of setting up changes on how patient results are processed in the office in order to prevent this from happening again to anyone. I'll offer any support he needs regarding my mistake. When we are both satisfied with the discussion, I would shift gears and focus on Mr. Diode's current medical condition.

Probing Questions

✓ How would you explain to Mr. Diode exactly what has happened?

✓ What are some consequences of being honest in this situation?

✓ How would you respond if Mr. Diode became angry?

✓ Describe in detail how you can prevent a recurrence of this nature in the future?

References

1. Hofmeister M. et al. The Acceptability of the Multiple Mini Interview for Resident Selection. *Residency Education* Nov-Dec 2008 734.

Please discuss with the interviewer your decision to pursue a career as a pharmacist.

In your answer, please include any relevant factor(s) that lead to your decision to apply to pharmacy school.

Pocket 1	*What general type of scenario does this MMI station fit into?*

Pocket 2	*What is the main problem or issue in this MMI station?*

Pocket 3	*What is the main source of the problem or issue in this MMI station?*

Pocket 4	*What personal experience do I have to include that is relevant to this MMI station?*

Pocket 5	*How would I resolve the problem or issue, taking into account my perspective and other perspectives for this MMI station?*

Answers to Pocket Questions

> Pocket 1: Traditional Interview category (why
> pharmacy?)
> Pocket 2: Discussing why you want to be a
> pharmacist.
> Pocket 3: Effectively being able to sell your story
> about why pharmacy to the interviewer.

In this MMI station, your perspective refers to your motivations for entering pharmacy and other perspectives refers to your thoughts for not wanting to enter other health professions. A strong, credible answer to this MMI station will allow the interviewer to clearly remember you from other interviewees. Your personal story if told correctly will make it obvious to the interviewer that you have placed significant emphasis and have undergone significant relevant experiences to adequately prepare you for a future career in pharmacy.

Why pharmacy and not another health profession?

Pharmacists interact daily with other health care professionals in multidisciplinary settings. The role of each health care professional is important in providing efficient, patient centered care.

Therefore, it is *just as important to be able to justify why other health care professions are not the best fit for you as it is to be able to confidently tell your interviewer why you want to go into pharmacy.* To help you formulate your answer, please keep in mind the ways pharmacy differs from other health professions and ask yourself *"how are these differences able to account for a better fit in my career choice as a pharmacist?"*

General approach

Even though "why pharmacy" is a highly personalized answer, a few general comments can be made about what makes an answer to why pharmacy "strong".

> ➤ A strong answer clearly identifies that the applicant has thought about other health care professions and has ultimately arrived at the conclusion that being a pharmacist is the career that best suits them.

> ➤ A strong answer clearly shows that the applicant clearly understands what the profession of pharmacy has to offer them and forms a strong bridge with their past experiences.

> ➤ A strong answer clearly portrays the applicant's interest in being a pharmacist chronologically in such a way that shows adequate preparation for a career in pharmacy.

Sample Model Response

Interviewer: "Can you please tell me about your decision to pursue a career as a pharmacist."

Applicant: "My decision to become a pharmacist is the result of all of my experiences. After learning about a few medications in my first aid class, I began to think about health care as a career option and I wanted to explore this further. Over the years, I've sought out experiences in different health professions and enjoyed them to a certain degree but the field that is most satisfying and the best fit for me is pharmacy. Being able to help people is not enough for me. Pharmacists are experts in the composition and knowledge of medications. I want a career that will allow me the flexibility to council patients on the drug treatments they are prescribed, as well as be an educator and also have the opportunity to participate in pharmaceutical development.

While volunteering with my local pharmacist, I observe the therapeutic relationship between pharmacists and the patients they council. I've also participated in drug development research in my undergrad and this non-clinical aspect of pharmacy was very rewarding for me. These are just a few of the experiences I've sought out which have helped further solidify my decision to apply to pharmacy school and become a pharmacist."

Probing Questions

- ✓ What will you do if you don't get into pharmacy school this year?

- ✓ What do you think is the most challenging aspect to being a pharmacist?

- ✓ What do you think is the most rewarding aspect to being a pharmacist?

- ✓ What do you think is the least rewarding aspect to being a pharmacist?

17: *A Not so Hot Evaluation*

Your dental school employs a peer assessment program that requires all 8 of your tutorial group classmates in your year to evaluate your performance in key areas on a numerical scale from **1 (low)** to **10 (high)**. At the end of your first year of dental school, you receive the following evaluation below:

Shows appropriate empathy towards patients:
7.4 (class avg = 7.8)

Encourages communication and collaboration:
8.2 (class avg = 8.2)

Acknowledges one's own limitations and skills:
6.9 (class avg = 7.9)

Discuss with the interviewer how you feel about these results and what your next steps would be.

Pocket 1

What general type of scenario does this MMI station fit into?

Pocket 2

What is the main problem or issue in this MMI station?

Pocket 3

What is the main source of the problem or issue in this MMI station?

Pocket 4

What personal experience do I have to include that is relevant to this MMI station?

Pocket 5

How would I resolve the problem or issue, taking into account my perspective and other perspectives for this MMI station?

Answers to Pocket Questions

Pocket 1: Traditional Interview category (Self-
Assessment/Evaluations/weakness)
Pocket 2: Subpar peer evaluation.
Pocket 3: Performing below the class average
(Empathy and Self-limitation areas).

Evaluations constitute an important forward
component for any learner. They are available in all
different shapes and sizes. Some are knowledge
based and others like this example are peer based. In
this scenario, you have scored below the class
average in the key areas of "empathy" and
"acknowledging your own limitations". These areas
are difficult to objectively assess at any educational
level due to their subjective nature and the lack of
validated guidelines.

Empathy Basics

Empathy is a fundamental concept that plays
an important role in facilitating quality health care.
It is defined as a person's ability to accurately sense
the patient's private world as if it were their own, but
without ever losing the "as if" quality. The four
key domains of empathy include cognitive, emotive,
moral and behavioral [1]:

➤ The *cognitive* domain refers to a person's
ability to identify and understand others'
perspectives and predict their thoughts.

> The *emotive* domain describes the ability to experience and share in others' psychological states.
> The *moral* domain refers to an internal altruistic drive that motivates the practice of empathy.
> The *behavioral* dimension refers to the ability to communicate empathetic understanding and concerns.

The take home message for the purpose of the MMIs is that despite knowing a lot about the components of empathy, we don't have a good reliable tool to measure empathy [2]. Therefore to improve your score in the area of empathy, it is critical to focus on improvement within the individual components of empathy.

Acknowledging Your Own Limitations

It may not be obvious when you first read the prompt that this is really a weakness question bundled into an MMI format. Acknowledging your own limitations is synonymous with being able to identify areas of weaknesses. However, recognizing your limitations isn't about signaling weakness or about admitting defeat. It's about empowering yourself to be more successful in your future endeavors.

When picking a weakness, the key is to pick a weakness that you have been able to make progress on. Be prepared and have at least 2 weaknesses ready to discuss. In the case of the MMIs, do not volunteer any personal weaknesses unless explicitly asked. Instead use "fictional" weaknesses that are relevant to the station. You may want to use a personal experience where you were able to help others overcome their weaknesses but the key is to not reveal your own weaknesses unless explicitly asked. Remember to put your best foot forward at all times.

Sample Model Response

Interviewer: "Can you please tell me how you feel about these evaluation results and discuss your next steps."

Applicant: "It's the end of my first year of dental school and I've just received peer evaluation scores in the domains of empathy, communications, and identifying my own limitations. I'm at the class average for communications but below the class average in the areas of empathy and acknowledging my own limitations. I feel disappointed at these results but I'm optimistic that I will be able to move forward and improve my performance in these areas for future evaluations. I'm also very appreciative of the feedback received from my peers in these domains. To improve my performance in the area of empathy, I would actively seek out feedback directly from my patients and my group members. In order to more effectively recognize my own limitations, I would first examine my own weaknesses in more detail and then seek out help from others to improve my performance in these areas. In terms of communications, I also want to see my performance improve further. I will reassess my own strengths, focus on non-verbal aspects of communication and increase my awareness of personal interactions. After taking all these measures, I would ask to receive evaluations at regular intervals to be able to better gauge my progress instead of waiting until the end of the academic year.

Probing Questions

- ✓ What does empathy mean to you?

- ✓ How would you monitor your results to ensure you are making progress?

- ✓ Are there any other individuals you would want to seek the help of?

- ✓ Where does time management fit into your action plan?

References

1. Morse JM. et al. Exploring empathy: a conceptual fit for nursing practice? *Journal of Nursing Scholarship.* 1992: 24(4), 273–280

2. Yu J. et al. Evaluation of empathy measurement tools in nursing: systematic review. *Journal of Advanced Nursing.* 2009 65(9), 1790–1806.

18: Practice Full Length MMI

General Interviewer Guidelines

Each applicant will have **two** minutes to read the scenario prompt. No more than two minutes should be allocated to read the prompt. At the end of the two minutes, the applicant should be given a minimum of **six** minutes to a maximum of **eight** minutes to complete the task identified in the scenario. Start the interview by asking them *"if they have had a chance to read the entire prompt?"* Do not interrupt the applicant while they are speaking. When they are finished giving their answer, please proceed with the probing questions. At the end of the station, complete the attached evaluation sheets and if interviewing multiple applicants, remember to assign each score only once for each category.

General Interviewee Guidelines

➢ Read the station prompt very carefully. You will have a maximum of **two** minutes to do so.
➢ Do not start your answer until instructed. You will have a maximum of eight minutes do complete the task.
➢ Repeat the process for the remaining stations.

Select sample model answers to the Practice Full Length MMI Scenarios that follow will be available on http://www.mmiprepbook.com starting in 2014.

-*Station 1* -

INSTRUCTIONS:

You have **two** minutes to read the following prompt. You will have **eight** minutes to complete the task indicated in the prompt below.
Do not enter the room until you are instructed to do so.

You are hired by the local zoo as an animal trainer to work with a new pair of chimpanzee monkeys. The zoo would like to set up an exhibit that allows the pair of chimpanzees to safely interact with the zoo visitors. This requires that the chimpanzees be fully trained and responsive to commands.

Upon meeting the pair of chimpanzees, you observe that they are very occupied and distracted. Despite offering treats, you are not able to get their full attention.

Please discuss with the interviewer your plan to succeed in training these two chimpanzees.

Probing Questions

- ✓ What will you do if you do not meet your deadline to have the chimpanzees trained?

- ✓ Are there any other individuals you would seek the help of to achieve your goal?

- ✓ What are some potential consequences of not meeting your deadline to have the chimpanzees trained?

- ✓ What would you say to your supervisor if you had to ask them for an extension?

MMI Scoring Sheet

Please rate the applicant's *overall performance* on this station *relative* to all applicants you are rating. Do not assign a score more than once (ie. if assessing 10 applicants, you may only use a score of 10 once). You may adjust your scores before submitting.

Consider the applicant's:
Ability to communicate effectively
Strength of the arguments displayed
Suitability for the program

Please place an "X" in the desired box below:

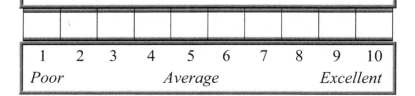

1	2	3	4	5	6	7	8	9	10
Poor				*Average*				*Excellent*	

Comments:

-*Station 2* -

You have **two** minutes to read the following prompt. You will have **eight** minutes to complete the task indicated in the prompt below.

Do not enter the room until you are instructed to do so.

You are a nutritionist working with a family doctor in your community. Along with the family doctor, you have formulated a care plan for a patient who was recently diagnosed with diabetes (type II). The patient is unaware that they have diabetes. Upon their return to see you, they feel great and ask for the results of their recent blood sugar testing.

Please discuss with the interviewer how you would proceed in this situation.

Probing Questions

- ✓ What are some relevant challenges to delivering bad news?

- ✓ In addition to the family physician, what other health care professionals are important in this patient's care?

- ✓ What will you do if the patient refuses to accept your care plan?

- ✓ Is it primarily the family doctor's responsibility to inform this patient of their diabetes diagnosis prior to seeing you?

MMI Scoring Sheet

Please rate the applicant's *overall performance* on this station *relative* to all applicants you are rating. Do not assign a score more than once (ie. if assessing 10 applicants, you may only use a score of 10 once). You may adjust your scores before submitting.

Consider the applicant's:
> **Ability to communicate effectively**
> **Strength of the arguments displayed**
> **Suitability for the program**

Please place an "X" in the desired box below:

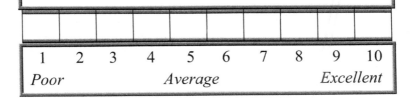

1	2	3	4	5	6	7	8	9	10
Poor				Average					Excellent

Comments:

-Station 3 -

You have **two** minutes to read the following prompt. You will have **eight** minutes to complete the task indicated in the prompt below.

Do not enter the room until you are instructed to do so.

You are a 4th year medical student doing your emergency medicine rotation. A 45 year old female struck by a vehicle while crossing the street has just arrived via ambulance and is in critical condition. She is unconscious but breathing on her own and has experienced significant blood loss. The ER nurse gets ahold of her husband and he is told to come to the emergency department immediately. As he arrives, both the senior medical resident and staff physician are busy keeping the patient alive. There is a possibility that she may not survive and they have asked you to have a brief discussion with the patient's husband to update him on his wife's current situation and to gather information about what should be done should her heart stop beating. The ER nurse tells you that her husband is waiting in the family room. You head towards the family room to meet him.

Please interact with her husband. During your encounter, please clarify her end of life wishes.

MMI Scoring Sheet

Please rate the applicant's *overall performance* on this station *relative* to all applicants you are rating. Do not assign a score more than once (ie. if assessing 10 applicants, you may only use a score of 10 once). You may adjust your scores before submitting.

Consider the applicant's:

      Ability to communicate effectively

      Strength of the arguments displayed

      Suitability for the program

Please place an "X" in the desired box below:

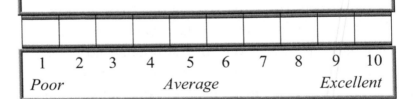

1	2	3	4	5	6	7	8	9	10
Poor				Average				Excellent	

Comments:

Station 4 -

You have **two** minutes to read the following prompt. You will have **eight** minutes to complete the task indicated in the prompt below.

Do not enter the room until you are instructed to do so.

The job is tough and you have fought your way up the ladder of success. You are working as an assistant manager for a large corporation and have been with the company for three years. The current manager of your department was promoted to her current position two years ago and after her promotion, "the power has gone to her head". She is overly demanding and has a "my way or the highway attitude". After a meeting, she approaches you and tells you that your job may be in jeopardy unless you can "see things eye to eye" with her.

Please discuss with the interviewer how you would respond to this situation?

Probing Questions

✓ What issues are most relevant to this scenario?

✓ If things did not improve at work, would you consider quitting?

✓ Is there any role for reporting the manager's behavior to higher authority?

✓ What are the risks associated with confronting your manager?

MMI Scoring Sheet

Please rate the applicant's *overall performance* on this station *relative* to all applicants you are rating. Do not assign a score more than once (ie. if assessing 10 applicants, you may only use a score of 10 once). You may adjust your scores before submitting.

Consider the applicant's:
Ability to communicate effectively
Strength of the arguments displayed
Suitability for the program

Please place an "X" in the desired box below:

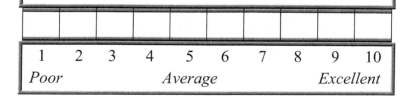

1	2	3	4	5	6	7	8	9	10
Poor				Average					Excellent

Comments:

-Station 5 -

You have **two** minutes to read the following prompt. You will have **eight** minutes to complete the task indicated in the prompt below.

Do not enter the room until you are instructed to do so.

Veterinarians must often accept that they will have to provide euthanasia to healthy animals. This contradicts the viewpoint that individuals enter veterinary medicine to save the lives of animals rather than to take lives. Euthanasia of healthy animals is an example of a concern among many practicing veterinarians.

Please discuss with the interviewer whether you agree with this concern. If applicable, please provide specific strategies to illustrate how you intend to address this concern.

Probing Questions

✓ What else might you do to address your concerns?

✓ Should euthanizing an otherwise healthy animal be outlawed?

✓ What would be the most challenging aspect of veterinary school for you?

✓ Is there anything else you'd like to add that we have not covered?

MMI Scoring Sheet

Please rate the applicant's *overall performance* on this station *relative* to all applicants you are rating. Do not assign a score more than once (ie. if assessing 10 applicants, you may only use a score of 10 once). You may adjust your scores before submitting.

Consider the applicant's:
  Ability to communicate effectively
  Strength of the arguments displayed
  Suitability for the program

Please place an "X" in the desired box below:

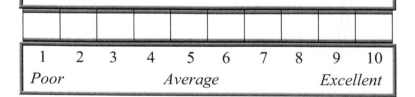

1	2	3	4	5	6	7	8	9	10
Poor				Average					Excellent

Comments:

-*Station 6* -

You have **two** minutes to read the following prompt. You will have **eight** minutes to complete the task indicated in the prompt below.
Do not enter the room until you are instructed to do so.

The proverbial phrase, "Tell me who your friends are and I'll tell you who you are" is used to represent the idea that like attracts like. A number of medical schools automatically grant admissions' interviews to applicants whose parents are former graduates and alumni of the program. As the newly hired dean of a medical school, a meeting with the members of the admissions' committee has been called to discuss whether the practice of automatically granting legacy interviews to alumni children should continue or cease to exist.

Please discuss with the interviewer whether you feel legacy interviews for alumni children should continue or cease to exist.

Probing Questions

✔ Describe the emotions you would feel if your desired outcome was not supported by the other members of the admissions' committee.

✔ What issues are raised by such legacy interview practices?

✔ What would you do to convince the admissions' committee to reconsider their decisions?

✔ How might legacy interviews affect the quality of the selected student body?

MMI Scoring Sheet

Please rate the applicant's *overall performance* on this station *relative* to all applicants you are rating. Do not assign a score more than once (ie. if assessing 10 applicants, you may only use a score of 10 once). You may adjust your scores before submitting.

Consider the applicant's:
> **Ability to communicate effectively**
> **Strength of the arguments displayed**
> **Suitability for the program**

Please place an "X" in the desired box below:

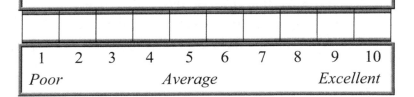

1	2	3	4	5	6	7	8	9	10
Poor				*Average*					*Excellent*

Comments:

-Station 7 -

You have **two** minutes to read the following prompt. You will have **eight** minutes to complete the task indicated in the prompt below.
Do not enter the room until you are instructed to do so.

A general observation in the pharmaceutical industry is that the consumer costs of prescription medications are significantly higher in the United States compared to other developed countries.

A principle to account for the differential cost of prescription medications among developed countries is that the United States bears the largest burden of drug research and development and subsequently must pass this burden on to US consumers.

Please discuss with the interviewer whether you think this principle is valid and/or acceptable.

Probing Questions

- ✓ Describe the ethical issue(s) raised by this pharmaceutical principle.

- ✓ Please explain what is more important, fairness to the individual or fairness to society?

- ✓ What possible suggestions could you employ to bring down the costs of medications in the United States?

- ✓ What are some possible consequences if the costs of prescription medications continue to rise in the United States?

MMI Scoring Sheet

Please rate the applicant's *overall performance* on this station *relative* to all applicants you are rating. Do not assign a score more than once (ie. if assessing 10 applicants, you may only use a score of 10 once). You may adjust your scores before submitting.

Consider the applicant's:

> **Ability to communicate effectively**
> **Strength of the arguments displayed**
> **Suitability for the program**

Please place an "X" in the desired box below:

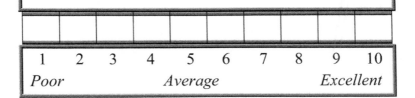

1	2	3	4	5	6	7	8	9	10
Poor				*Average*					*Excellent*

Comments:

-Station 8 -

You have **two** minutes to read the following prompt. You will have **eight** minutes to complete the task indicated in the prompt below.
Do not enter the room until you are instructed to do so.

In 2012, the American Academy of Family Physicians published an article exploring the impact of physician role models. They used scenarios involving physicians offering smoking cessation and lifestyle counseling to their smoking patients. According to the authors' research, patients have more confidence in preventive health counseling advice from non-smoking physicians compared to their smoking counterparts. The study also concluded that physicians with medically unhealthy personal lifestyle habits are less likely to counsel their patients about adopting a healthy lifestyle.

Please discuss with the interviewer whether physicians have a duty to act as healthy role models for their patients.

Probing Questions

- ✓ What factors determine whether someone is a role model?

- ✓ What are the implications of unhealthy lifestyle habits such as obesity that readily manifest themselves more easily?

- ✓ What are some possible limitations of the research study conducted?

- ✓ Is a physician obligated by society to take good care of their health?

MMI Scoring Sheet

Please rate the applicant's *overall performance* on this station *relative* to all applicants you are rating. Do not assign a score more than once (ie. if assessing 10 applicants, you may only use a score of 10 once). You may adjust your scores before submitting.

Consider the applicant's:
Ability to communicate effectively
Strength of the arguments displayed
Suitability for the program

Please place an "X" in the desired box below:

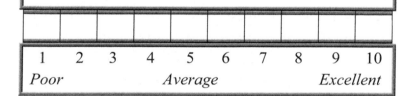

1	2	3	4	5	6	7	8	9	10
Poor				Average				Excellent	

Comments:

-Station 9 -

You have **two** minutes to read the following prompt. You will have **eight** minutes to complete the task indicated in the prompt below.

Do not enter the room until you are instructed to do so.

The Health Premium (HP) is a component of many provinces' Personal Income Tax system - the revenue generated is applied to health care spending. The HP is based on taxable income for a taxation year. The premium charged ranges from $0 - $900 annually. Currently, individuals with total taxable incomes of less than $20,000 do not have to pay this premium whereas individuals with total taxable incomes of greater than $200,000 have to pay a $900 premium. Research suggests that a disproportionate amount of health care costs result from spending on individuals with taxable incomes of less than $35,000. As the Health Minister, you are asked to respond to a bill that would require everyone to pay an equal premium regardless of their personal income.

Based on the above results, please discuss with the interviewer what will you include in your response?

Probing Questions

- ✓ What general principles would you apply to justify your response?

- ✓ Please explain what is more important, fairness to the individual or fairness to society?

- ✓ Is the balance between individual fairness and societal needs different where the medical profession is concerned?

- ✓ Would you ultimately support this bill?

MMI Scoring Sheet

Please rate the applicant's *overall performance* on this station *relative* to all applicants you are rating. Do not assign a score more than once (ie. if assessing 10 applicants, you may only use a score of 10 once). You may adjust your scores before submitting.

Consider the applicant's:
Ability to communicate effectively
Strength of the arguments displayed
Suitability for the program

Please place an "X" in the desired box below:

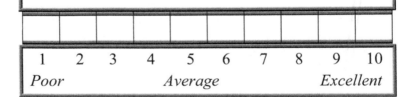

1	2	3	4	5	6	7	8	9	10
Poor				Average				Excellent	

Comments:

-*Station 10* -

You have **two** minutes to read the following prompt. You will have **eight** minutes to complete the task indicated in the prompt below.
Do not enter the room until you are instructed to do so.

You are a child support worker for child protection services and receive an anonymous call from a concerned neighbor regarding a case of suspected child abuse. She tells you that a couple and their two younger children, ages 9 and 13, have recently moved into the apartment next door to her. She has noticed several bruises on the children's faces along with poor hygiene. When she questions the children directly in front of their parents, they seem reserved and unwilling to talk and say the bruises are a result of their own carelessness.

Please discuss with the interviewer how you would respond to this call?

Probing Questions

✔ Describe the ethical issue(s) raised by this scenario.

✔ Are there any additional individuals you would involve?

✔ What are some immediate physical and emotional consequences of abuse?

✔ What are some long term physical and emotional consequences of abuse?

MMI Scoring Sheet

Please rate the applicant's *overall performance* on this station *relative* to all applicants you are rating. Do not assign a score more than once (ie. if assessing 10 applicants, you may only use a score of 10 once). You may adjust your scores before submitting.

Consider the applicant's:
      Ability to communicate effectively
      Strength of the arguments displayed
      Suitability for the program

Please place an "X" in the desired box below:

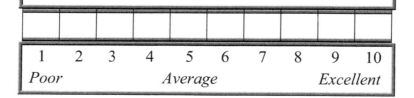

1	2	3	4	5	6	7	8	9	10
Poor				*Average*				*Excellent*	

Comments:

Part 3
The Extras

19: Programs that currently use the MMI

The following medical, pharmacy, dental and veterinary schools now employ the MMI as part of their admissions' process. The list was compiled November 2013 and continues to grow daily.

Medical Schools – United States & Canada

State	School Name
Arizona	University of Arizona College of Medicine (Tucson)
	University of Arizona College of Medicine (Phoenix)
	A.T. Still University of Health Sciences, School of Osteopathic Medicine (Mesa) **DO**
California	David Geffen School of Medicine at UCLA
	Stanford University School of Medicine
	University of California - Davis School of Medicine
	University of California - Riverside School of Medicine
	University of California - San Diego School of Medicine

	University of California - Irvine School of Medicine
	Western University of Health Sciences College of Osteopathic Medicine of the Pacific **DO**
Indiana	Marian University College of Osteopathic Medicine **DO**
Massachusetts	University of Massachusetts Medical School
	Tufts University School of Medicine – (Maine Track)
Michigan	Michigan State University College of Human Medicine
	Central Michigan University College of Medicine
	Western Michigan University School of Medicine
Missouri	University of Missouri-Kansas City School of Medicine
Mississippi	University of Mississippi School of Medicine
New Jersey	Cooper Medical School of Rowan University
	Rutgers, Robert Wood Johnson Medical School
	Albany Medical College
	State University of New York

State	School Name
New York	(SUNY) Upstate Medical University College of Medicine
	New York University School of Medicine
	New York Medical College
North Carolina	Duke University School of Medicine
Ohio	University of Cincinnati College of Medicine
Oklahoma	University of Oklahoma College of Medicine
Oregon	Oregon Health & Science University School of Medicine
Puerto Rico	Universidad Central del Caribe School of Medicine
Virginia	Virginia Tech Carilion School of Medicine (Roanoke)
Washington	Pacific Northwest University College of Osteopathic Medicine (Yakima) **DO**
Province	School Name
Alberta	University of Alberta Faculty of Medicine and Dentistry (Edmonton)
	University of Calgary Faculty of Medicine

British Columbia	University of British Columbia Faculty of Medicine
Manitoba	University of Manitoba Faculty of Medicine (Winnipeg)
Newfoundland	Memorial University of Newfoundland Faculty of Medicine (St. Johns
Nova Scotia	Dalhousie University Faculty of Medicine (Halifax)
Ontario	McMaster University Michael G. DeGroote School of Medicine (Hamilton)
	Northern Ontario School of Medicine (Thunder Bay)
	Queen's University Faculty of Health Sciences (Kingston)
Quebec	Laval University Faculty of Medicine (Quebec City)
	McGill University Faculty of Medicine (Montreal)
	University of Montreal Faculty of Medicine
	University of Sherbrooke Faculty of Medicine
Saskatchewan	University of Saskatchewan College of Medicine

Pharmacy Schools – United States & Canada

State	School Name
California	University of California – San Francisco School of Pharmacy
Colorado	Regis University School of Pharmacy (Denver)
Florida	University of South Florida School of Pharmacy
Illinois	University of Illinois at Chicago College of Pharmacy
Kentucky	Sullivan University College of Pharmacy (Louisville)
	University of Kentucky College of Pharmacy (Lexington)
Oklahoma	University of Oklahoma College of Pharmacy (Oklahoma City)

Province	School Name
British Columbia	University of British Columbia Faculty of Pharmaceutical Sciences (Vancouver)
Ontario	University of Toronto Leslie Dan Faculty of Pharmacy
Nova Scotia	Dalhousie University College of Pharmacy (Halifax)

Dental Schools – United States & Canada

State	School Name
Florida	LECOM College of Dental Medicine (Bradenton)
Illinois	Midwestern University College of Dental Medicine- Illinois (Downers Grove)
Michigan	University of Michigan School of Dentistry (Ann Arbor)
Mississippi	University of Mississippi School of Dentistry (Jackson)
Ohio	Ohio State University College of Dentistry (Columbus)
Province	School Name
Saskatchewan	University of Saskatchewan College of Dentistry (Saskatoon)

Veterinary Medical Schools – United States & Canada

State	School Name
California	University of California - Davis School of Veterinary Medicine
Maryland	Virginia-Maryland Regional College of Veterinary Medicine
Oregon	Oregon State University College of Veterinary Medicine
Texas	Texas A&M University College of Veterinary Medicine & Biomedical Sciences (College Station)
Virginia	Virginia-Maryland Regional College of Veterinary Medicine
Province	**School Name**
Alberta	University of Calgary Faculty of Veterinary Medicine
Ontario	University of Guelph Ontario Veterinary College

- ➢ Show up at least 35 minutes earlier than your scheduled time.

- ➢ _**Always**_ ask the interviewer a question when prompted "do you have any questions?"

- ➢ Do not ramble on in your answer for more than _**TWO**_ minutes at a time. Pause and assess for body language/cues.

- ➢ Read everything _**carefully**_ and remember to always follow instructions!

- ➢ Do your background reading about the program/city/institution ahead of time.

- ➢ Show confidence in your answers but respect that everyone will have weak points, including yourself.

- ➢ For traditional interviews ask ahead of time for your interviewers' names and google them if possible.

- ➢ For MMI interviews, be familiar with the interview structure ahead of time.

- ➢ Don't read more into the question/scenario then there really is.

- ➢ Don't leave your interview preparation until the last minute.

- ➢ Go into the interview with the attitude that your hard work will pay off and that you will get into the program for which you are interviewing.

About the Author

Kevyn To, M.D., is an admissions consultant and the founder of Advisor Prep Education Services (www.advisorprepfor.me). A graduate of the State University of New York, Upstate College of Medicine, he began admissions consulting as a medical student in Syracuse, New York and has since helped many applicants succeed in obtaining admission to top medical schools, competitive specialties, top residency and fellowship programs. After completing medical school, he pursued residency training in Radiation Oncology at the Juravinski Cancer Center and Princess Margaret Cancer Center.

He was among the first participants in the original pilot M.D. program Multiple Mini-Interview (MMI) circuits at McMaster University School of Medicine in 2003 and has previously served as an admissions' MMI interviewer and CASPer (Computer-Based Assessment for Sampling Personal Characteristics) assessor for the M.D. program, Michael G. DeGroote School of Medicine at McMaster University.

In addition to possessing extensive knowledge about the MMI and traditional interview processes, he has also served as a reviewer for McGraw Hill Medical and is a former recipient of the American Medical Association Foundation, Excellence in Medicine and Leadership Award.

CPSIA information can be obtained
at www.ICGtesting.com
Printed in the USA
LVOW04s2155290116

472894LV00025B/756/P